Ankylosaurus is pronounced: an-**kie**-low-saw-rus

To Hugh Lyon
—**K. W.**

Atheneum Books for Young Readers
An imprint of Simon & Schuster Children's Publishing Division
1230 Avenue of the Americas, New York, New York 10020
Text copyright © 2003 by Karen Wallace
Illustrations copyright © 2003 by Mike Bostock
First published in London in 2003 by Hodder Children's Books, a division of Hodder Headline Limited
All rights reserved, including the right of reproduction in whole or in part in any form.
The text of this book is set in Bumpers.
Manufactured in Hong Kong
First U.S. Edition, 2005
2 4 6 8 10 9 7 5 3 1

CIP data for this book is available from the Library of Congress.
ISBN 0-689-87318-2

Consultant: Dr. Angela Milner, Head of Fossil Vertebrates Division
of Paleontology, the Natural History Museum, London

I Am an
Ankylosaurus

WRITTEN BY **Karen Wallace**

ILLUSTRATED BY **Mike Bostock**

Atheneum Books for Young Readers
New York London Toronto Sydney

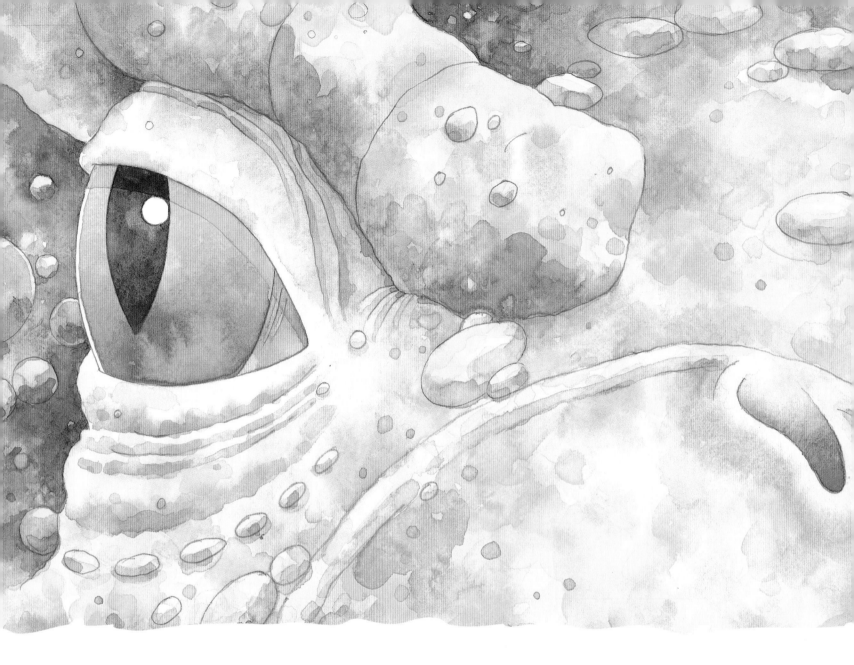

I am an ankylosaurus.

I am plodding over warm sand.

Look through my eyes and see what I see.

A mother ankylosaurus
crosses a dry riverbed.
Lizards scuttle in front of her.
A snake slithers past her.

The ankylosaurus plods onward.
She needs to lay eggs.

A mother
ankylosaurus digs
a nest in the sand.
It is shallow and wide.

Other ankylosauruses dig
their own nests beside her.
When her nest pit is finished,
she turns around and around in a circle.
Each time she turns, an egg drops in the sand.

A watchful ankylosaurus
stands by her nest.
She's huge like a tank.
She is covered in armor.
Bony plates join together
under her skin.
Stubby spikes grow
all over her body.
Her spiky tail ends
in a club made of bone.

Slow-moving ankylosaurus!
Her bones make her heavy.
Even her eyelids and nose
have bones to protect them.

As she turns in the sand,
a troodon sneaks up behind her.
He's quick and he's clever.
He wants ankylosaurus eggs.

Angry
ankylosaurus!

She smells the troodon's scent.

As he leaps on her nest,

she slams her tail sideways.

The club flies through
the air like a ball of iron.
She smashes the troodon
and the egg in his claws.

Hungry ankylosaurus!

She plunges into the forest.

Above her head, giant trees stretch up to the sky.

At her feet, shiny plants are crowded together.

Wide-mouthed ankylosaurus!
Her jaws grind together.

She rips ferns.
She grinds twigs.
She eats whole spiky bushes.
A huge ankylosaurus
chews a path through
the forest.

Months follow months.
Tadpoles turn into frogs.
Glittering dragonflies emerge in the sunshine.

The mother ankylosaurus crosses the riverbed.
Her eggs are ready to hatch in their
nest of warm sand.

The baby ankylosauruses
crack open their shells.
Hundreds of others are
hatching around them.
They creep over the sand
and into the forest.
They nibble green leaves
and hide in the shadows.

The mother ankylosaurus
plods down to the lake shore.
Her young ones have grown now.
She slurps the cool water.
She doesn't smell the
tyrannosaurus as he runs
from the forest.
He claws at her belly.
She stumbles and falls.

I am an ankylosaurus.

I roll back to my feet.

I slam my tail sideways.

Bone smashes bone.

The tyrannosaurus limps away.
The battle is over.